21 Days with God

God

Prayers for victory, provision and promises

Dr. Amanda H. Goodson

ISBN-13:978-0997875713

ISBN-10:0997875712

Printed in the U.S.A.

First Edition

Acknowledgements:

Thank You, God, for allowing me to serve You in such a manner as is pleasing to You. I pray that I will find favor in Your sight as I share these stories with others and that they may also be blessed. I am grateful for my family, for their dedication to me, and all that God has allowed me to do.

Thank you, to Diane Snell for being a significant contributor to this ministry effort.

TABLE OF CONTENTS

Introduction

INTRODUCTION

God's heart rests with those who seek a sincere relationship and have a passionate desire to be in fellowship with Him. From the moment that God gave us His breath of life, we have the opportunity to experience oneness with Him. The very depth, height, and width of God is a demonstration of the capacity of His love. His love is without limits, and it is available to all who desire to reside in His loving care.

This book, *21 Days with God,* comprises a daily journey of revelation through prayer, into that place where we can become one with God and reach a place where we find divine comfort, access, healing, and results. Every believer desires to be able to pray better and become comfortable doing so. This daily walk will gently guide the reader in taking a practical and applicable journey of relationship-building in order to reach that goal. The intent of this book is that the reader be able to accomplish this by utilizing relevant stories that demonstrate how we live and how we are made better because of a true relationship with Jesus Christ our Savior.

It isn't always necessary to use flowery phrases and poignant prose in our prayers in order for us to hear the voice of God, and conversely, to be heard. We can be direct and simple and still be fully in His presence. Matthew 18:3 teaches us to pray with the heart of little children; that is, our prayers should be simple, reverent, specific, and trusting. Simple, in that our prayers should be presented with a spirit that is humble and yet straightforward. Reverent, in that we must always come before God in a way that is respectful and with a spirit of worship. Specific, in that we should be clear in stating precisely what the prayer references. Trusting, in that we are to fully believe and know that God is who He says He is, and that He will do precisely what His Word promises He will do.

I invite you to take this daily journey and to see how your life can and will be transformed through prayer. It is guaranteed that, through a daily commitment to prayer, your life will be changed, your relationship with God will be enhanced, and you will see the difference that this makes in your life.

Day 1 – The Breath of God

This is the account of the heavens and the earth when they were created, when the LORD God made the earth and the heavens.

Scripture:

Now no shrub had yet appeared on the earth and no plant had yet sprung up, for the LORD God had not sent rain on the earth and there was no one to work the ground, 6 but streams came up from the earth and watered the whole surface of the ground. 7 Then the LORD God formed a man from the dust of the ground and breathed into his nostrils the breath of life, and the man became a living being.

(Genesis 2:5-7)

Story:

Marion enjoyed sharing the biblical creation story to her intermediate Sunday school class. Her class was always intrigued and attentive when she would announce the lesson of the day with such joy and excitement. On this Sunday she had captured their attention by proclaiming aloud this simple statement: "Now I will tell you about the greatest love story known to mankind. It is about God and His love for humanity. God," she explained, "is the giver of life. He showed His love for us when He breathed life into Adam's nostrils on the sixth day of creation. God breathed out His spirit into the dust of the earth which He had gathered to form man. With his very act of God, man had become a living (breathing) creature."

"Close your eyes," she exclaimed. "Now, inhale and imagine God breathing out every time you breathe in. It is the breath of life which we cannot live without!" She would exclaim, "We are always attached to God. Man cannot create man, nor can man breathe life into any creature without God first creating it and giving it life. Man can, through artificial means, help sustain life, but he cannot create it. Any additional questions," she would chirp (as the class time dwindled to zero), "please ask your parents!"

For those of us who are parents this breathing is the long awaited response during the birthing process that lets us know that our child has arrived in this world. We wait for the cry of our newborn child to signal that life has begun. The child is now a living breathing being; not because we breathed into it, but because God did. That shrill of a cry lets us know that our child has "breathed in" the breath of air that God continued to supply to all mankind beginning with His first interaction with Adam.

This breathing is a requirement for sustained life. When God breathed into Adam's nostrils, He set into motion a system of events that are necessary for sustaining every human being. Humans, and all humanity everywhere, are dependent upon this breath of life, which is a continuous process from life's beginning to its end. We have a rate at which we breathe daily. Our breathing rate is easily determined. Just to give you an idea of the number of times you breathe per day (within a year, or in a life time), count the number of times you breathe in a minute, then multiply that by the number of minutes in a day, and you might breathe 50,000 times or more per day. In a month or a year, the number would be astronomical!

There is a second breath that we accredit to God that also has a powerful impact on our lives. It is known as scripture. According to 2 Timothy, all scripture is God breathed and is useful for teaching, rebuking, correcting, and training in righteousness. It too, is life supporting and allows us to grow in spiritual maturity in the knowledge of God.

We humbly submit our thanks to God who gave us through His breath, both life and the instructional scriptures that help us develop mature relationships with Him through His Word.

Prayer:

Father, God, we stand in reverential awe of the first life-giving breath that You breathed into Adam's nostrils. With it, all humanity came to life (through Your breath) and relies upon Your Word (scripture) to maintain every physical and spiritual need. Amen.

Ready to Write:

Record your thoughts and reflections on *The Breath of God*, Genesis 2:5-7, and the prayer. Consider what it means to have God's very breath flowing through your body each moment of your life.

Today's Date:

_____
_____
_____
_____
_____
_____
_____
_____
_____
_____
_____
_____
_____
_____
_____

The Breath of God

Humans, and all humanity everywhere, are dependent upon God's breath of life.

Day 2 – The Depth of God

The scripture accounts the depth to which God has gone to honor His covenant with humanity. We are witnesses to the true Word of God and His keeping of the covenantal promises.

Scripture:

After the reading from the Law and the Prophets, the leaders of the synagogue sent word to them, saying, "Brothers, if you have a word of exhortation for the people, please speak."
16 Standing up, Paul motioned with his hand and said: "Fellow Israelites and you Gentiles who worship God, listen to me! 17 The God of the people of Israel chose our ancestors; he made the people prosper during their stay in Egypt; with mighty power he led them out of that country; 18 for about forty years he endured their conduct in the wilderness; 19 and he overthrew seven nations in Canaan, giving their land to his people as their inheritance. 20 All this took about 450 years. "After this, God gave them judges until the time

of Samuel the prophet. ²¹ Then the people asked for a king, and he gave them Saul son of Kish, of the tribe of Benjamin, who ruled forty years. ²² After removing Saul, he made David their king. God testified concerning him: 'I have found David son of Jesse, a man after my own heart; he will do everything I want him to do.' ²³ "From this man's descendants God has brought to Israel the Savior Jesus, as he promised. ²⁴ Before the coming of Jesus, John preached repentance and baptism to all the people of Israel. ²⁵ As John was completing his work, he said: 'Who do you suppose I am? I am not the one you are looking for. But there is one coming after me whose sandals I am not worthy to untie.' ²⁶ "Fellow children of Abraham and you God-fearing Gentiles, it is to us that this message of salvation has been sent. ²⁷ The people of Jerusalem and their rulers did not recognize Jesus, yet in condemning him they fulfilled the words of the prophets that are read every Sabbath. ²⁸ Though they found no proper ground for a death sentence, they asked Pilate to have him executed. ²⁹ When they had carried out all that was written about him, they took him down from the cross and laid him in a tomb. ³⁰ But God raised him from the dead, ³¹ and for many days he was seen by those who had traveled with him from Galilee to Jerusalem. They are now his witnesses to our people. ³² "We tell you the good news: What God promised our ancestors ³³ he has fulfilled for us, their children, by raising up Jesus.

(Acts 13:15-22)

Story:

Bill had a wonderful way of describing the depth of scriptures. Simply put, the scriptures are as deep as the ocean or maybe the Grand Canyon. Have you have ever stood on the rocky rim of the canyon and looked down into its vast opening? It is a visual depiction of the depth to which God went to let you know that you should never lean on your own understanding, but believe God that His Word is true. "This truth," Bill would say, "shall set you free. Do not lean to your own understanding but in all things through prayer and supplications with thanksgiving make your request known to God." Then Bill would top the conversation with another scripture: "For your ways are not God's ways."

"How, then, are we supposed to understand the deep things of God?" someone would ask. Bill would always answer, "By faith." "What then is the depth of God's relationship with us?" another would ask. Then Bill would answer, "That, too, is based on your faith and your obedience to the Word of God."

"From Genesis to Revelation, God's Word remains true and consistent. God is not a man that He should lie nor the son of man that He should repent. His Word is, and has always been, truth and life to humanity," Bill would explain.

Scripture lends to our knowledge that God keeps His promises as He gave them to the prophets for His chosen people. God hears the outcry of those who believe, and He answers them. The true depth of God's love is understood by His covenant promised to all mankind. Salvation, redemption, and forgiveness of sin are all ours, for God's love knows no limits for all creation. These opportunities are afforded to all believers. His grace and mercy are immeasurable. There is a "renewing" in these times to the discipleship of Christ: those who have ears let them hear what says the Lord our God to His people.

Prayer:

God, teach us to accept the love that You have for us and to reciprocate that love to You and to all mankind. Amen.

Ready to Write:

Record your thoughts and reflections on The Depth of God, Acts 13:15-22, and the prayer. Consider what it means that the scriptures are as deep as the ocean.

Today's Date:

_____
_____
_____
_____
_____

The Depth of God
The Scriptures are as deep as the ocean.

Day 3 – The Height of God

Scripture:

After six days Jesus took with him Peter, James and John the brother of James, and led them up a high mountain by themselves. ² There he was transfigured before them. His face shone like the sun, and his clothes became as white as the light. ³ Just then there appeared before them Moses and Elijah, talking with Jesus. ⁴ Peter said to Jesus, "Lord, it is good for us to be here. If you wish, I will put up three shelters—one for you, one for Moses and one for Elijah." ⁵ While he was still speaking, a bright cloud covered them, and a voice from the cloud said, "This is my Son, whom I love; with him I am well pleased. Listen to him!" ⁶ When the disciples heard this, they fell facedown to the ground, terrified. ⁷ But Jesus came and touched them. "Get up," he said. "Don't be afraid." ⁸ When they looked up, they saw no one except Jesus.

(Matthew 17:1-8)

Story:

Gwendolyn shared stories about laying on her back and gazing into the sky thinking of how Jesus had transfigured before His disciples. She imagined His face shining like the sun and His clothes becoming as white as light. She understood the limitations of depth and height within the physical realm, but knew that the love God had for her had no such limitations. These were created things, and as such were not able to separate God's love from her.

She also pondered the return of Christ to take the world and God's people from Satan forever. There was no doubt of what God was capable of doing, nor His reason for doing so. His Word had been given by the prophets and is outlined in scripture. There was no doubt in her mind that God had said it, and that God would do what He said.

Prayer:

Lord, teach me to trust with the heart of a child that the depths of Your love for me has no boundaries. Amen.

Ready to Write:

Record your thoughts and reflections on *The Height of God*, Matthew 17:1-8, and the prayer. Consider that there is no limit to where God's love can reach.

Today's Date:

_____
_____
_____
_____
_____
_____
_____
_____
_____
_____
_____
_____
_____
_____
_____
_____
_____
_____
_____
_____
_____
_____

The Height of God

The love of God for you has no limitations.

Day 4 – The Width of God

Scripture:

Praise the LORD, my soul; all my inmost being, praise His holy Name. [2] Praise the LORD, my soul, and forget not all His benefits—[3] who forgives all your sins and heals all your diseases, [4] who redeems your life from the pit and crowns you with love and compassion, [5] who satisfies your desires with good things so that your youth is renewed like the eagle's. [6] The LORD works righteousness and justice for all the oppressed. [7] He made known his ways to Moses, His deeds to the people of Israel: [8] The LORD is compassionate and gracious, slow to anger, abounding in love. [9] He will not always accuse, nor will He harbor His anger forever; [10] He does not treat us as our sins deserve or repay us according to our iniquities. [11] For as high as the heavens are above the earth, so great is His love for those who fear Him; [12] as far as the east is from the west, so far has He removed our transgressions from us.

(Psalm 103:1-12)

Story:

Imagine thinking that the earth is flat. It is hard to believe that this was the theory that limited some travelers years ago. The frightening idea was that if they traveled too close to the edge of the world, they might fall off was a true threat of man.

To early travelers this was a real fear that imposed limitations as to where they could travel. Beyond the horizon was an unknown that could end in tragedy if one traveled beyond the earth's boundary. How far one could safely travel to get to that boundary was not known. Yet for believers, God knew and God could separate us from our sins with this imaginary distance.

God is limitless, and His ability to function in time and space is without limit and without fear. How wonderful the psalmist is to remind us that the Creator of the universe was never limited by His creations. God has no physical or spiritual limitations. His great compassion and grace are given without limitations to those whom He loves. In return, we move beyond our human limitations because of the compassion and grace that God freely gives to all humanity.

Often when flying across the world to distant cities, I will peer out of the small airplane window at the world that God has allowed me to traverse, and sit in awe of the limitless beauty of the world I view from high above its surface.

The beauty of the earth can be seen in photographs taken in space far above the earth's surface. The wonder of God's galactic creation is so grand that it transcends thought that His love for humanity is not bound by any physical or spiritual limitation. It is across this great distance that our sins are separated from us.

We have grace and favor, we have salvation, and we are redeemed. Accepting the redemptive work of Jesus on the cross frees us to love God and one another. Sin shall not limit this love, for Jesus has set the example and–overcoming sin–has given all the choice of obedient love that frees us to love God as He loves us.

This is the greatest love story ever to be told, and it continues to unfold daily. There is no greater love than the love of God for His creation. It is an open invitation to repent and turn from the fallen ways of man and to return the true limitless love of God. This love is given to all without limit. The invitation is open, and no one who receives Jesus as Lord and Savior is omitted. No sin (save one) can keep mankind away from the love of God. The sting of sin has been taken away by Christ.

Today and every day we are invited into the arms of God. Seek and you shall find the limitless love of God.

Prayer:

God, without limits, I have accepted Your love for me. I have chosen to repent and turn from sin and return to You. I confess with my mouth that Jesus is my Lord and Savior. You are love, and I am loved. Amen.

Ready to Write:

Record your thoughts and reflections on *The Width of God*, Psalm 103:1-12, and the prayer. Consider that your confessed sins are thrown into the sea of forgetfulness, removed from you as far as the east is to the west.

Today's Date:

_____
_____
_____
_____
_____
_____
_____
_____
_____
_____
_____

The Width of God

Your sins are separated from you by the width of His love.

Day 5 – God is for You

Scripture:

What, then, shall we say in response to these things? If God is for us, who can be against us? 32 He who did not spare his own Son, but gave him up for us all—how will he not also, along with him, graciously give us all things? 33 Who will bring any charge against those whom God has chosen? It is God who justifies. 34 Who then is the one who condemns? No one. Christ Jesus who died—more than that, who was raised to life—is at the right hand of God and is also interceding for us. 35 Who shall separate us from the love of Christ? Shall trouble or hardship or persecution or famine or nakedness or danger or sword? 36 As it is written: "For your sake we face death all day long; we are considered as sheep to be slaughtered." 37 No, in all these things we are more than conquerors through him who loved us. 38 For I am convinced that neither death nor life, neither angels nor demons, neither the present nor the future, nor any powers, 39 neither height nor depth, nor anything else in all creation, will be able to separate us from the love of God that is in Christ Jesus our Lord.

(Romans 8:31-39)

Story:

"GREATER IS HE THAT IS IN ME THAN HE THAT IS IN THIS WORLD."

"I wrote this scripture on everything that I own. It is above my future title on my bedroom wall." Celeste proudly admits this to everyone who ventures into her territory and asks the question of who she is to become in her later life. She is a high school senior who has found the love of Jesus, and she knows that with Him on her side, she can do all things. Her destiny has been strategically planned for the next 50 years of her life. The words below the scripture read "Reverend Dr. Celeste Moore; Harvard class of 2019; Dr. of Pediatric Medicine."

What great dreams she has for her future. It was not always this way and the road to her future wound around a few of the curves she had been thrown in life. An absentee mother was how she described Janet to other students. Mom had missed the bus several years ago and had not participated in her daughter's life. She knew she had a dad. That was an undisputed biological requirement for creating a life. Exactly who the lucky man was had never been determined or discussed between her and the grandmother that raised her. Grandma was a praying, bible-toting, Sunday school teaching, extra-large, soft-spoken woman. Celeste was her joy. God had given Celeste a grandma to love her and that was quite all right with the two of them. It did Grandma's heart well to hear Celeste talk about her future, and financially, both she and Grandma knew that God would have to provide the educational funds. And they both knew, without a doubt, that God could.

Celeste knew all the bible stories. For years her mantra was, "If God be for us, who can be against us." She prayed often that God would be for her, for often God was the only "for her" in her life. Several seasons she had asked God to answer a harder question she often faced, "Who is man that you are mindful of him." Why would God care about her when He had so many others as options? When she came to the conclusion that God had shown His love for her when He had given His only begotten Son as a last sacrifice for all sin, she knew she was the apple of His eye!

Celeste believed that Jesus was Lord and Savior of her life. Jesus had paid a heavy price for her life, and she could not love Him more or thank Him more than to become His ambassador.

The love of God was no strange request for her. She knew God loved her because He had given her a grandmother, a church family, and Kingdom inheritance, and made her an ambassador of His Word.

She took great joy in sharing the Word of God with others. She knew the calling on her life would ultimately place her in a ministry leadership role, and she relished the idea. God had kept His end of the deal. "If God is for us," she would often tell her grandma, "who then can be against us." Conquering the world was something God has arranged for her to do.

Prayer:

We are absolutely, positively, without a doubt, certain that Your love is capable of sustaining us through this life. Thank you. Amen.

Ready to Write:

Record your thoughts and reflections on the truth that *God is for You*, Romans 8:31-39, and the prayer. Consider that if no one else in the world seems to be on your side, God is and always will be.

Today's Date:

_____
_____
_____
_____
_____
_____

God is for You
With God on your side, you can do all things.

Day 6 – God is with You

Scripture:

Now the king of Aram was at war with Israel. After conferring with his officers, he said, "I will set up my camp in such and such a place." ⁹ The man of God sent word to the king of Israel: "Beware of passing that place, because the Arameans are going down there." ¹⁰ So the king of Israel checked on the place indicated by the man of God. Time and again Elisha warned the king, so that he was on his guard in such places. ¹¹ This enraged the king of Aram. He summoned his officers and demanded of them, "Tell me! Which of us is on the side of the king of Israel?" ¹² "None of us, my lord the king," said one of his officers, "but Elisha, the prophet who is in Israel, tells the king of Israel the very words you speak in your bedroom." ¹³ "Go, find out where he is," the king ordered, "so I can send men and capture him." The report came back: "He is in Dothan." ¹⁴ Then he sent horses and chariots and a strong force there. They went by night and surrounded the city. ¹⁵ When the servant of the man of God got up and went out early the next morning, an army with horses and chariots had surrounded the city. "Oh no, my lord! What shall we do?" the servant asked. ¹⁶ "Don't be afraid," the prophet answered. "Those who are with us are more than those who are with them." ¹⁷ And Elisha prayed, "Open his eyes, Lord, so that he may see." Then the Lord opened the servant's eyes, and he looked and saw the hills full of horses and chariots of fire all around Elisha. ¹⁸ As the enemy came down toward him, Elisha prayed to the Lord, "Strike this army with blindness." So he struck them with blindness, as Elisha had asked. ¹⁹ Elisha told them, "This is not the road and this is not the city. Follow me, and I will lead you to the man you are looking for." And he led them to Samaria. ²⁰ After they entered the city, Elisha said, "Lord, open the eyes of these men so they can see." Then the Lord opened their eyes and they looked, and there they were, inside Samaria. ²¹ When the king of Israel saw them, he asked Elisha, "Shall I kill them, my father? Shall I kill them?" ²² "Do not kill them," he answered. "Would you kill those you have captured with your own sword or bow? Set food and water before them so that they may eat and drink and then go back to their master." ²³ So he prepared a great feast for them, and after they had finished eating and drinking, he sent them away, and they returned to their master. So

***the bands from Aram stopped raiding Israel's
territory.***

(2 Kings 6:8-23)

Story:

Today our enemies may be the strongholds to which
we have given control over our lives. And often we feel
surrounded without a way out. But this feeling of
helplessness (physical or spiritual tribulation) is never
true; it's only perceived. When thinking about spiritual
warfare, it is great to have a team of prayer warriors
ready for battle.

I am reminded of a Pastor who was determined to
take back the block on which her church stood. She
walked the neighborhood and felt sure that the church
had much to offer but was located in a drug-infested
part of town where most people would not want to
visit, let alone call their church home.

Slowly she began to get to know the people who call
this section of town their home. She used the limited
funds that she had to clean up the area around the
church. With the help of 2 or 3 people who bravely
came to church on most Sunday mornings, they began
to expand on their clean up efforts to include local
housing areas and schools. Her ministry grew when
more people who were interested in helping with the
cleanup would venture past their own protected
houses.

The neighborhood was changing. The church was growing. As the neighborhood became more active, the drug activity began to subside. Police and law officials became noticeable and active. Prayer was her weapon of choice. Like Joshua she went to the battleground taking God with her. She prayed over every house, over every yard, every child, and every family whether they belonged to her church or not. She invited others throughout the city to join her in making her request known to God. She opened the church doors to anyone and everyone who would come seeking God. She opened the church to the community as a safe haven from drugs and drug dealers.

Slowly the people began to return to the church. The education programs began to blossom as the drug programs began to disappear. She suffered personal loss of her car, and the church furniture but did not let any of that deter her from her God-given task. God expanded her territory and gave her victory as he had given Joshua. She marched around her territory in faith that, "If God be for us, then who can be against us." God was present in her fight for this community and slowly began to show her the fruit of her labor. The fight is not over still, but at least in the spiritual realm, there God has already given her the victory. When we come together in prayer, God hears our prayers and answers us.

Prayer:

God, we step forward in prayer and supplication to offer ourselves as living sacrifices standing on Your Word to increase our territory. We know that "if You are with us," no one can defeat us when the weapons of our fight are not carnal. Amen.

Ready to Write:

Record your thoughts and reflections on the truth that *God is with You*, 2 Kings 6:8-23, and the prayer. Consider that You never go into any battle, natural or spiritual, alone.

Today's Date:

_____
_____
_____
_____
_____
_____
_____
_____
_____
_____
_____
_____
_____
_____

God is with You

You never have to face anything alone because God is with you.

Day 7– The God in You

Scripture:

Don't you know that you yourselves are God's temple and that God's Spirit dwells in your midst.

(1 Corinthians 3:16)

Story:

In bible study Fred often reminds us that we are "the Kingdom of God" and that we "smell like Christ." The scripture for this section reminds me of the many times when people have come up to me and said that they can see the "Spirit of God all over me." What an honor!

Bethany always reminds the other members of the women's ministry that where two or more are gathered, Jesus said He would be there also. God in our midst is a great honor. She apologizes for nothing because we should always acknowledge God. Our language, our acts, everything we do should reflect who we are in Christ. I am humbled by the opportunity to represent God. I am thankful that he has chosen me to do the work of the ministry. I believe that God is alive and actively working through us to reach others. I most humbly consider myself a "Kingdom representative, an ambassador of the Most High God."

Prayer:

Let the redeemed of the Lord say so in word and in deed. Thank You for being our God and allowing us to call ourselves children of the Most High God. May we always well represent You. Amen.

Ready to Write:

Record your thoughts and reflections on *The God in You*, 1 Corinthians 3:16, and the prayer. Consider that you are a representative of God, His presence, and His Kingdom.

Today's Date:

_____

_____

_____

_____

_____

_____

_____

_____

_____

The God in You

Everything you do and are reflects who you are in Christ.

Day 8 – The Protector

Scripture:

There is no one like the God of Jeshurun, Who rides the heavens to help you, And in His excellency on the clouds. The eternal God is your refuge, and underneath are the everlasting arms.

(Deuteronomy 33:26)

Story:

We often think of the Psalms of David when talking about God as our protector. The wonderful narratives of the Old Testament Bible offer many examples of how God protected the nation of Israel and gave them victory over their enemies. Those stories help us understand the power of God in doing this same thing for us.

When the enemy seems to take for granted that they are more powerful or more ruthless, God steps in and takes care of the believers, the children of Israel, His chosen ones. News flash, the Gentiles have been engrafted into the kingdom through Christ, and now we all can turn to God as our refuge in times of trouble. The trouble is not always some great army. Today our enemies and our troubles may not need thousands of warriors to come to our defense.

Gideon defeated a mighty army with only 300 men. What you should know is that God can be your refuge from all kinds of trouble. Don't put limits on what God can do or what you can do through God's working in your life. There is no problem too large or too small for God. Submission and obedience should be attributes of your relationship with God. Prayer is a mighty weapon that opens you up to the protection of God in all areas of your lives.

I am often reminded of a friend who came home when a burglar was leaving her house. She wasn't so worried about what he had taken for in obedience to God she was returning from a trip to the bank where she had just deposited her precious jewelry in a steal box for protection. Her most valuable heirlooms were safely tucked away with her bank account information and money. She knew that what he found in her house was not worth her confronting him. God had provided for her safety by allowing her to arrive as he left.

She watched patiently taking pictures and calling the police. She could provide them with photographic evidence of his intrusion and his departure. "It doesn't always work out this way," the policeman had reminded her. "Most people know their robbers, but the encounter is often messy."

The story is unique. The man was caught and convicted by the person he was robbing. She was on God's time frame and was protected by God's arrangement of the unfolding events.

Prayer:

God, You are my on time, in time, all time, protection. I will listen to Your voice and heed Your instruction. May others find refuge and protection from trying trials and tribulations in You. Amen.

Ready to Write:

Record your thoughts and reflections on God as *The Protector*, Deuteronomy 33:26, and the prayer. Consider that that God is able to protect you from any enemy.

Today's Date:

_____
_____
_____
_____
_____
_____

The Protector

We can turn to God as our refuge in times of trouble.

Day 9 – The Provider

Scripture:

But my covenant I will establish with Isaac, whom Sarah shall bear to you at this set time next year." *22Then He finished talking with him, and God went up from Abraham.*

(Genesis 17:21-22)

Story:

Some hold to the idea that when the Lord provides, it must be in a material format. In this scripture, God had promised Abraham an heir through his son Isaac. The promises of God are not always material in nature. Oftentimes God provides for us a deeper understanding of His Word or a more intimate relationship with Him. We cannot put a material value on such great gifts.

On several occasions, I have had people thank me for increasing their understanding or knowledge of a "Word" when they listen to the messages God has

55

given me to share. We often call this "validation" of the Word of knowledge, or foretelling, or a forth telling of events received from God.

The Word is often a powerful tool to be utilized in any given situation. Often hearers will say that God spoke to them through the Word proclaimed. It may not be a prophecy to them (although that can happen), but a verification or validation of the Word.

In this same scripture God says of Ishmael, I have heard you (Abraham). Behold, I have blessed him and will make him fruitful, and will multiply him exceedingly." The words proclaimed in sermon messages are constructed to do the same.

Not only will God provide your non-material needs, God will provide your material needs too! Meet Betsy. Betsy, a church member, recently shared how she had prayed for God to change her financial situation. She was not able to meet her monthly financial obligations. God had instructed her to increase her giving beyond her normal level but how could she do that when she was already unable to pay her debts. The message shared that Sunday was on trusting God, and giving above and beyond; not just in finances, but in the talents that God has gifted us to have. Giving knowing that God would give to her with the measure in which she gave.

She decided the message contained the confirmation that that she needed. She would trust God. Over the next few weeks she added a prayerful expectation to her giving and increased her activity in the church. Her testimony today is about how God not only provided a financial blessing to meet her need, but opened her eyes up to the talents she could share with the church in the form of an administrative talent. Her fruit was utilized in assisting with answering the church phone, a task the church greatly needed to have handled. God provided by multiplying her financial situation so that she was not lacking in her ability to meet her financial obligations.

Prayer:

Your mercy and grace are sufficient in my life allowing me to serve You to the fullest of my ability. Open the eyes of my understanding so that I'm assured that You are a God of abundance. Amen.

Ready to Write:

Record your thoughts and reflections on *The Provider*, Genesis 17:21-22, and the prayer. Consider that the truths that have been validated for you, and partner with God to have your needs met.

Today's Date:

_____
_____
_____

The Provider

When you invest your talents into God's work, He'll return an increased harvest that provides your every need.

Day 10 – The Priest

Scripture:

Now this is the main point of the things we are saying: We have such a High Priest, who is seated at the right hand on the throne of the Majesty in the heavens. ² A minister of the sanctuary and of the true tabernacle which the Lord erected, and not man. ³ For every high priest is appointed to offer both gifts and sacrifices. ⁶ But now He has obtained a more excellent ministry, inasmuch as He is also Mediator of a better covenant, which was established on better promises.

(Hebrews 8:1-3)

Story:

This is the beginning scripture for the "New Priestly Service" describing Jesus as the High Priest of God. It is the beginning of the Hebrews discussion of Jesus and the covenant of the "Good News."

It would be redundant to say that all who receive Jesus as Lord are included in this covenant. With this covenant a new way was begun. The ultimate sacrifices for sin had been paid. Acceptance and repentance were now the order of the era.

Quite often I encounter people who say they are not ready for "rebirth" through Christ. I am thankful that Jesus did not change His mind about the work He had to do on the cross.

As His disciples in this age, we are to tell everyone of God, about the work of Jesus Christ, and about the indwelling ascension gift of the Holy Spirit. We are the people of God. God will do the work in them.

"For I will be merciful to their unrighteousness, and their sins and their lawless deeds I will remember no more."

(Hebrews 8:12)

It is this "New Covenant" that allows us to be saved by grace.

A new convert once asked, "What if I forget or I slip up or I return to my old ways." It was humbling to respond that, "You have no *old* ways because you have been reborn in Christ. Your old ways are forgiven." She asked the same question the next week. "Slipping into my old ways is hard," she would say. What I began to notice is that as she became engaged in the Word and the work of the church, her 'slipping up' confessions became fewer and farther apart.

62

One day she proclaimed to me that she had engaged friends in conversations about God's forgiveness and acceptance of her without conviction and it had changed her life. She now had a testimony of the goodness and love of God that has changed her life. Jesus, as her High Priest interceded for her. Our merciful God had patiently waited on Anna to turn from her lost ways to find love in Him.

Prayer:

Father, we thank You for the redemptive work of Your loving Son that continues to allow us to humbly turn to You for salvation and deliverance. Amen.

Ready to Write:

Record your thoughts and reflections on *The Priest*, Hebrews 8:1-3, and the prayer. Consider that God has given you new life through this New Covenant.

Today's Date:

_____
_____
_____
_____
_____
_____
_____
_____
_____
_____

The Priest

The sacrifice for sins has been fully paid, so once you repent you are accepted. Jesus interceeded for you.

Day 11 – The Prince of Peace

Scripture:

For unto us a Child is born, Unto us a Son is given: And the government will be upon His shoulder. And His name will be called Wonderful, counselor, Might God, Everlasting Father, Prince of peace.

(Isaiah 9:6)

Story:

It is the peace of God that surpasses all understanding that we find in turning from sin unto Christ. We find our purpose in the Word of God and an inner peace in the knowledge of whose we are.

How often do we fight against the unknown wiles of the destroyer only to find that when we turn to Christ, our situations and our lives change?

Kill, steal and destroy are the weapons of Satan. He tried to get Christ to yield to his becoming in the desert encounter. When we face trials we must remember to whom we (born-again believers) belong. One weapon of the destroyer is strongholds. Satan uses anger, envy, and depression as ways to get us to submit to his will. Church going, repented believers will not yield to the whispering of Satan's strongholds.

Dana, often confesses that she has a temper and when someone gets on that last nerve, she explodes. Often without asking for strength to hold her tongue, she lashes out in anger. In an effort to surprise her for her 39th birthday, her husband Ben planned a surprise party. Everyone knew that she had no clue as to what he was planning. He invited her closest friends to join them at a posh local restaurant. On the evening of the event, a girlfriend leaked that she was meeting Ben for dinner. Dana overheard the conversation. Without question she planned to meet them at the restaurant and let them both have it! She arrived at the restaurant in an angry rage!! Screaming and yelling at everyone in her path not noticing that her few close friends were there also. She continuously screamed false accusations at Ben. She accused him of cheating amongst other things. He could not quiet her down as she (without candor) lashed out at her friend.

Once the dust had settled and most of her "past" embarrassed friends had left the restaurant, she sat ashamed of her actions. Satan had taken her mistrust of Ben and multiplied it beyond what her few friends could withstand. On this day she learned the power of an unbridled, angry tongue.

She and Ben survived the evening of terror, but many of the old friends did not. Counseling has taken her to a place of understanding and peace that she had not known. The peace of God that quells the fiery darts of the adversary. The lies that once defeated her attempts at control, have lost their power. She understands the need to control her temper. For perfect peace is hers when she controls her heart and mind and focuses on God.

Prayer:

Let the meditations of my heart and mind be focused on God at all times. Let me treat others with the kindness and dignity that I want from them. God, be the center of my joy and my life. Allow me to love as I am loved. Amen.

Ready to Write:

Record your thoughts and reflections on *The Prince of Peace,* Isaiah 9:6, and the prayer. Consider that Christ gives you peace and love that conquers anger and other emotions.

Today's Date:

_____

_____

_____

The Prince of Peace

When trials come, knowing who you are in Christ will allow you to maintain a life of peace.

Day 12 – The Covenant from God

Scripture:

***Behold, the days are coming, says the Lord when
I will make a new covenant with the house of
Israel and with the house of Judah.***

(Jeremiah 31:31)

Story:

The covenant which we are currently under, is the
covenant of grace. Through Jesus Christ, God has
made this New Covenant.

A covenant is defined as a contract between two
parties. It is a legal agreement holding both parties
responsible to act according to laws and bylaws of that
contract.

When I took my new job I entered into a contract with
my employer, as many do. My contract is based on
supply and demand. For a fee, I agreed to supply and

apply myself to meet the company needs, and in turn, the company would respond with monetary awards. The contract is sealed with my signature and that of the company representative.

The "New Covenant," between God and believers, was sealed by God and the redemptive work of Jesus Christ. Believers receive redemption, deliverance, and salvation! What a contract! All are saved by grace through faith.

Prayer:

God, thank You for being faithful to Your Word. We know that because You are faithful, we are confident of being sealed by Your blood through the redemptive work of our Savior, Jesus Christ. Amen.

Ready to Write:

Record your thoughts and reflections on *The Covenant from God*, Jeremiah 31:31, and the prayer. Consider that the benefits of knowing God are yours by contractual right.

Today's Date:

_____
_____
_____

The Covenant from God

God's covenant is signed by Jesus Christ, our Savior, and allows for salvation by grace through faith.

Day 13 – The Covering of God

Scripture:

Be imitators of me, as I am of Christ. *³ I want you to understand that the head of every man is Christ, the head of a wife is her husband; the head of Christ is God.*

(1 Corinthians 11:1, 3)

Story:

Deborah found it difficult to submit to her husband and always states that this is an old school belief. To this I can retort, "This is new testament scripture. God is a God of order."

When Deborah began to have problems in her marriage, the marriage counselor suggested she try to submit to the will of God as outlined in this scripture. This required making a change in her beliefs and her way of thinking. She began to see her husband

William in a new light and their marriage took on a meaning that it had not had before.

Her submission was to the will of God. Her understanding was enlightened as to the role of her husband as her covering. Her honoring him as such changed their interactions and how they treated each other. She often admits this new way of thinking is contrary to her old independent ways. And she will add, she is enjoying the new relationship she has, not only with her husband, but in their matrimonial walk with God.

Prayer:

God, show me how to submit to authority as Jesus did. Not thinking that it is demeaning, but that it is loving to submit to the will of God for my life, my family, and my church. Amen.

Ready to Write:

Record your thoughts and reflections on *The Covering of God*, 1 Corinthians 11: 1, 3, and the prayer. Consider that God covers you as a husband covers a wife.

Today's Date:

_____
_____
_____
_____

The Covering of God

Submitting to God's will and authority gives us His protection and confidence to submit to others without fear.

Day 14 – God as My Father

Scripture:

***Our Father in heaven; hallowed be Your Name.
(Matthew 6:9)***

Story:

In teaching us how to pray, Jesus also taught us to call upon God as "our Father." Fatherhood announces that the male of our society has taken on the role of parent.

New fathers are wonderful to watch. I admire watching male friends pass out pens to let the world know that they have become fathers. In our society, it is common to see new fathers pushing strollers and taking care of their children.

Adam, a friend, often meets up with his best friend Jarred (and his children) for outings with his daughter Cindy. Adam takes an active role in his daughter's life as coach, homework instructor, and direct care provider.

God takes this same role in the lives of believers. He loves so much more that we could ever imagine. As the Creator of all things, He is our Father, Provider (Jehovah Jireh), our Counselor, and our Protector. The greatest act of love is recorded in John 3:16 when He gave His only begotten Son because of His love for us.

God, our heavenly father is holy and loves us with an everlasting love.

Prayer:

Father, God, thank You for allowing us to give ourselves over to You in Prayer. Your Kingdom come, Your will be done; on earth as it is in heaven. Amen.

Ready to Write:

Record your thoughts and reflections on *God as My Father*, Matthew 6:9, and the prayer. Consider that the Creator of the universe is your Father and loves you infinitely.

Today's Date:

_____
_____
_____

God as My Father
God's love for us is that of a perfect Father.

Day 15 – Jesus is my Lord

Scripture:

If you confess with your mouth and believe in your heart that Jesus is Lord, then you shall be saved.

(Romans 10:9)

Story:

Luke had heard the invitation to join his church as a repented Christian on several occasions. However, today he was actually listening for understanding, wanting to know what is was that the newly re-born Christian was signing up to do. The confession was easy enough to repeat with little difficulty. What Luke had not expected was the struggle he had repeating these words. He had been baptized and joined church many times over the years and now he had a desire to understand exactly what he had confessed doing.

His expectation was that something miraculous was supposed to take place with this confession. He believed and accepted Jesus as his Lord and Savior, but was not quite sure he was ready to fully commit to working in the church. Luke's pastor took the time to explain the meaning of confessing his sin and acknowledging his being born again spirit, just as Jesus had explained it to Nicodemus.

With a full understanding of the repentance process, Luke could now enjoy his time with his family. The term 'lord' means owner, and in terms of being a landlord, the meaning refers to one who owns the building. Luke understood that at the moment he became saved, redemption and salvation were his.

Prayer:

Lord Jesus, I confess that you are Lord over my life. Grant that I may get to know You and expand my relationship with You as a Spirit-filled child of the Most High God. Amen.

Ready to Write:

Record your thoughts and reflections on *Jesus is My Lord*, Romans 10:9, and the prayer. Consider that confession and heart belief begin your relationship with Jesus Christ.

Today's Date:

_____
_____
_____
_____
_____
_____
_____
_____
_____
_____
_____
_____
_____
_____
_____
_____
_____
_____
_____
_____
_____

Jesus is My Lord

Jesus saves us and has the right to be Lord over our lives.

Day 16 – The Holy Spirit is My Seal

Scripture:

It is God who makes both us and you stand firm in Christ. He anointed us, set his seal of ownership on us, and put his Spirit in our hearts as a deposit, guaranteeing what is to come.

(2 Corinthians 1:22)

Story:

The seal of the Lord is permanent and everlasting. God sealed His covenant with Abraham by swearing upon Himself, for He could find none greater by which to seal it.

It is a wonderful sight when the Spirit of God fills the sanctuary. As children, we loved being in church when the Holy Spirit of God would fill the room.

Baptism is the sacrament that seals the converted Christian into his new walk with Christ. Most believers know the events of the day when they were baptized. Mark describes his with humor. He announces proudly that he had to be "dunked at least 3 times" at the discretion of his Pastor.

The "spiritual" sealing took place on the day of Pentecost for the new apostles and the new church. The seal of God is His Holy Spirit. Being "sealed' of God means that we belong to God, that God is our Father, and that have we received His covenant graces. Ephesians 1:13-14 states that we are sealed in God with the Holy Spirit of promise who was given as a pledge of our inheritance. This holy act seals us as sons of Almighty God. Our inheritance is the Kingdom of God. The Spirit of God now indwells us to empower and equip us for ministry.

Prayer:

Thank you, God, for the gift of the Holy Spirit that is our seal. We accept the Holy Spirit as our Comforter, our Instructor, and our Intercessor. Amen.

Ready to Write:

Record your thoughts and reflections on *The Holy Spirit is My Seal*, 2 Corinthians 1:22, and the prayer. Consider that you fully belong to God and have His power inside of you.

Today's Date:

_____

The Holy Spirit is My Seal
We are sealed unto salvation by God's Holy Spirit.

Day 17 – When God is for me, I Win

Scripture:

No temptation has overtaken you except such as is common to man; God is faithful, who will now allow you to be tempted beyond what you are able, but with the temptation will also make a way of escape, that you may be able to bear it.

(1 Corinthians 1:13)

Story:

We know the outcome of the final battle between Christ and Satan. We, the children of God, know that 'we win.' Chris, a new convert to the Christian way of life, is often heard saying that the knowledge of the outcome of the final battle Satan wages against the children of God and Christ is the greatest secret not kept. His past history included drugs, and as he states it "every conceivable wrong that man can commit." One cold, drug-filled day, about six (6) months ago,

Chris heard what he believed was the voice of God speaking to him about forgiveness and love. He boldly tells anyone and everyone that he believes in his heart that God spoke to him about changing his ways and life through repentance and love. He walked into the church crying and asking for forgiveness which he did not immediately receive.

The congregation welcomed him with open hearts. They had welcomed him many times before. But this time Chris was adamant that he had come because God had invited him. And this time he had come to stay.

The road back from the wicked life he had led was not to be an easy one, but one he did not have to take alone. Today his story is a testimony that changes many lives. No one he told congratulated him on leaving his past life, and no one has volunteered to exchange their lives with him. Chris found his strength in God.

There are many living his old life to whom he can tell of a new way through Christ. He does so without haste; wanting to lead them God. Chris knows that he has won!

Prayer:

Thank you, God, for the victory. We win! We live day to day knowing the power of Your love to grant us salvation and eternity. Amen.

Ready to Write:

Record your thoughts and reflections on *When God is for Me, I Win*, 1 Corinthians 1:13, and the prayer. Consider that God can deliver and keep you from your past.

Today's Date:

_____

_____

_____

_____

_____

_____

_____

_____

_____

_____

_____

_____

_____

_____

_____

_____

_____

_____

_____

_____

_____

_____

When God is for Me, I Win

With God on our side we win in life and in the days to come.

Day 18 – God as my Healer

Scripture:

Bless the Lord, O my soul and all that is within me, bless his holy name! ² *Bless the Lord, O my soul and forget not all his benefits* ³ *who forgives all your iniquity, and heals all your diseases.*

(Psalm 103:1-3)

If my people, who are called by my name, will humble themselves and pray and seek my face and turn from their wicked ways, then I will hear from heaven, and I will forgive their sin and will heal their land.

(1 Chronicles 7:14)

Story:

When disaster strikes on a national level we rally to supply aide and resources to those affected. During this time, disease and sickness may increase. The gathering of the body of Christ in providing aid to others is a phenomenal act of kindness.

Samuel was caught up in hurricane Katrina, but felt he was too blessed to complain about his poverty. When he returned to what had been his home, he found only rubble and non-repairable trash. So, he packed what he had and started out for Texas. His hope was in God. God would take care of him until he could find work and repair his life. He wasn't too proud to ask for help, but he knew there were others with a greater need. Alone and hungry he began his trek to find a new life.

Samuel talked to God with every step. "Lord, You said if I obey and humble myself, then You would heal my land. Father, I place my life in Your protective care. I am willing to work for what You deem meets my needs." In his travels, he met others with greater need and gave to them what he had earned; often it was not more than a sandwich.

Samuel hungered not for the food that feeds the flesh, but that which feeds the spirit. The greatest gift he received was a weathered Bible found amongst a heap of rubble. He felt that it had come directly from God to keep him company during the long, heated nights. Most often it was his companion and his food in times of struggle.

In Texas, Samuel was able to find some work, volunteering his services as a cook in a homeless shelter. He found the work to be a powerful pill for reparation. Slowly he was able to build on his life. What Samuel had learned from his endeavors was that he did not need as much in material possessions as before.

One day he looked around at what he had gained from the fruit of his labors. God had met Samuel right in the middle of his condition and had taken care of him. He didn't have much, but he felt wonderful because he realized that he didn't need much! God had met his promise of care as He had told Samuel not to worry about tomorrow. Samuel kept God at the forefront of his recovery.

Samuel felt a need to return to his home. He knew there was not much more than trash that had gathered on the site when he walked away earlier. Samuel reminded God that He had promised to heal the land, sickness and diseases around him. One morning he woke up bright and early, and started his walk back to his home. He eventually worked his way back home.

Samuel stood in the vacant lot that had been his home humbled himself, sought and called out to God. Your servant has returned Lord. He knew the work would be tedious, but felt God has blessed his hands to rebuild the home he so dearly missed. He had begun the work, with little more than a prayer and a promise.

His prayer had worked! He learned that the disaster relief sent need medicine and doctors to help with the sick and needy in the community. And also, help to rebuild his home.

Prayer:

First, God, rebuild us that we may serve You in heart, mind, spirit, and soul. Bless Your servants, that we may build that which pleases You, God. Thank you for healing our sicknesses, diseases and our land. Amen.

Ready to Write:

Record your thoughts and reflections on *God as My Healer*, Psalm 103:1-3, and the prayer. Consider that God promises to heal all that needs to be healed in your life.

Today's Date:

_____
_____
_____
_____
_____
_____
_____
_____
_____

God as My Healer
God's ability and desire to heal includes every area of life–mind, body, soul, and land.

Day 19 – God, my Salvation

Scripture:

Surely God is my salvation; I will trust and not be afraid. The Lord is my strength and my defense; he has become my salvation." [3] With joy you will draw water from the wells of salvation.

(Isaiah 12:2-3)

Story:

Olivia often speaks of how the Lord was her Rock in time of need. She faced the loss of her husband in a car accident, the loss of her job, and with it every material possession she owned. As she describes it "I lost everything I once valued." But she says it with a smile and a conviction that God brought her through these tough times to take her to a higher place in Him.

Ask her how she can still flash that beautiful smile, and her only answer is, "God was my Defense. He was my saving grace to give me what I need to make it though. I called upon him day and night, and He heard my cry. He delivered me from the devil and allowed me to rest in His peace." Then with all conviction she adds, "God is my Savior. He would not let me see ruin. He had another path for me to take; one where I would have to totally rely on Him. When I realized that the one thing I could not lose was the love of God, then I knew that he had kept me from total self-destruction. Now, God is my Joy and my Rock, my Salvation…my Defense. I recommend Him to everyone I know, and I celebrate His love daily."

Prayer:

In you, God, I put my trust. My love for You is greater than self-centeredness. I will sing and shout with joy of Your love for me always. Amen.

Ready to Write:

Record your thoughts and reflections on *God, My Salvation*, Isaiah 12:2-3, and the prayer. Consider that God's salvation extends beyond rescue from sin.

Today's Date:

_____
_____
_____
_____
_____

God, My Salvation

Trusting God in every circumstance gives us opportunities to experience His salvation over and over again.

Day 20 – God Will Never Leave Me Alone

Scripture:

Be strong and of good courage, do not fear nor be afraid of them; for the LORD your God, He is the One who goes with you. He will not leave you nor forsake you.

(Deuteronomy 31:6)

Story:

Pat shared this excerpt from his journal which he wrote during troubled times.

December 2010
In our times of trial and tribulation, we take notice to the loneliness of being by ourselves. We think that the world does not know or does not care about our problems. We must face each new problem and each new trial or tribulation not on our

own, but with the love and guidance of God. No one has gone through our specific situation.

Often we do not want advice; we want answers. When I was injured in the car accident, I thought not being able to walk or care for myself was the end of life as I knew it. Now having lost my ability to walk, I, Pat was dependent on the kindness of strangers. God had a different plan for me. Life had changed, but not for the worse; it had actually become better. The accident that was supposed to leave me bitter and angry had allowed me to see life from a very different angle.

Pat would share his story with others and add a very surprising twist. "God altered the outcome. Thinking that I would be alone for the remainder of my life, I was surprised to meet Kate. She was someone to whom the old Pat would not have given the time of day. I thought I was alone for life. I had believed in God in an earlier time in my life.

Kate had a strong bible-centered relationship with God. She was instrumental in showing me that God had not forgotten nor forsaken me. She had told me (over and over again) that God had not forgotten me. That was central to my recovery. Her love for me and God's love for me was what I needed to endure many painful nights. Kate knew that, with Christ, we are never alone; no matter what our circumstances may be."

It is a given and open promise that we all call upon in the varied seasons of life. Through fellow believers and her faith in God, Kate introduced Pat to a future filled with love and strength in the healing power of God.

Prayer:

I accept Jesus as the Lord and Savior of my life. Thank You, God, for being with me through every situation. I AM NEVER ALONE! You are there. Amen.

Ready to Write:

Record your thoughts and reflections on *God Will Never Leave Me Alone*, Deuteronomy 31:6, and the prayer. Consider that no matter you see or think, God never leaves you alone.

Today's Date:

_____
_____
_____
_____
_____
_____
_____
_____
_____
_____
_____

God Will Never Leave Me Alone

When we look for God during trials and tribulations we find, and realize we're not alone.

Day 21 – I Have Victory in Jesus

Scripture:

> ***Thanks be to God! He gives us the victory through our Lord, Jesus Christ.***
>
> ***(1 Corinthians 15:57)***

Story:

One of the most terrifying times in Ana's life came when she found herself facing a medical diagnosis that could have, and is often known to have, life-terminating consequences. She described hearing the words flow from the doctor's mouth as, "a terrifying experience in itself." His demeanor alone let her know that the conversation was not going to be pleasant for either of them.

Here is the outline of her testimony:

113

"His face was laced with sorrow and his voice stern, yet commanding. He was commanding me to move past my emotions to handle a situation my mind had not yet comprehended the possible positive outcomes, just the negative effects of many friendly outside encounters. I had listened to those dreaded words spoken by friends about their lives but never fathomed that I would hear them spoken over my own.

I heard the doctor speak, but his muffled voice came forward as if he had entered a time warp. My comprehension had left me, my ears were dumbed, and my heartbeat slowed down as if the whole world around us had entered a time warp zone or maybe the Twilight Zone. I watched as the sci-fi movie played out before me. In the days ahead I expected to hear Rod Sterling say, 'You have entered the twilight zone.'

There were additional tests to run and results to confirm. I felt that I had to be strong, not share until the confirmation came. In the days ahead, I talked with God about all the times He had been there for me and my family. He had gotten us through illness, and accidents before this would not be different.

I had leaned heavily on Him when my mother had suffered heart problems, and often when my mother-in-law had suffered breathing problems. I was leaning on my faith for others and now I prayed for his intervention on my behalf.

This scripture became my affirmation: *"He will not leave nor forsake me."* Because I knew it to be true.

On many occasions the Lord had gone before me. He had held me up in times of crisis. I had found rest in His presence and love in His grace. I had attested to His healing power and love many times through the trials of my life. This time was no different. My faith had never been based on what He had done for me, but on what He had done through His creation.

Weeks passed before the results were complete. Test after test, conversation after conversation, I placed my faith in Him. I already knew the results of one test– the test of my faith. I knew that victory over the enemy was mine, in Christ Jesus. That test I would pass. My life and my healing was in the hands of my Savior.

Total and complete trust of God is to be given, for He is Lord and Savior to all. Jesus' endurance for our sake bought us again into relationship with God. A price was paid. It was no little feat and it required total submission and obedience to God.

The test results that led to my dread were turned around through my faith. The doctor was amazed when the results showed no traces of a disease."

We have the victory through Christ. God is still healing His children.

Prayer:

Almighty God, Creator of all things made; we bring to You, Your Word spoken over all mankind that You will never leave or forsake us. In love we submit to You and are committed and commanded by You. For us, Your Word is sufficient. I have the victory in Christ Jesus, my Lord. Amen.

Ready to Write:

Record your thoughts and reflections on *I Have Victory in Jesus*, 1 Corinthians 15:57, and the prayer. Consider that God is able to turn every battle into a victory.

Today's Date:

_____
_____
_____
_____
_____
_____
_____
_____
_____
_____
_____
_____
_____

I Have Victory in Jesus

God saves us from sin and death so that we can live a life of victory!

CONCLUSION

Like love, prayer is an imperative–we are commanded to pray, just as we are commanded to love. Becoming a person of prayer is to fulfill your obligation to reaching and sustaining a true relationship with God. It was the expectation that this book, *21 Days with God*, would be the catalyst to assist you in effecting that change.

When we know God's plan through prayer, but we fail to practice it, then we are just like the person that is spoken of in James 1:22-25; we can see our reflection when looking into a mirror, but as soon as we turn away from that mirror, we forget what we look like. We were created in the image and likeness of God. We should, therefore, be a reflection of what He looks like and who He is. The only way to fully know what that looks like is to be in a committed relationship with Him and faithfully follow His Word through prayer and practice. Turning away from God and not desiring to be in His presence through prayer, is just like turning away from a mirror; it puts us in a place where we forget what we look like.

My challenge to you is that you will take this book and consistently begin praying according to the Word of God and in the Name of Jesus. Discover your power and authority, and discover that as you grow in prayer, your rights as an intercessor will also begin to grow. You *will* become a powerful individual of prayer.

ABOUT THE AUTHOR

Dr. Amanda H. Goodson

Amanda is an author, educator, facilitator, inspirational speaker and coach for corporations, agencies and non-profit organizations. Amanda inspires others and connects with her audiences by sharing real-life experiences using enthusiastic, energizing, and interactive methods. Amanda has a Bachelor's of Science in Electrical Engineering, a Master's of Science in Management, and a Doctor of Ministry Church Administration.

For further information or to book Dr. Goodson please contact her at:
AmandaGoodson.com

Books by Dr. Amanda Goodson

Spiritual Quickbooks ™
Kingdom Character
Spiritual Authority
Carmel Voices
The Power to Make an Impact
Powerful People Follow Christ
Step out in Faith
Going Higher, Declarations for Kids
On the Rise
Spiritual Intelligence
Switch to Holiness
12 Power Principles for Kingdom Leaders

Leadership Minibooks ™
The Authority of a Leader
Character of a Leader
Unlock Your Full Potential
12 Power Principles for Administrative Professionals
Soar to Your Destiny

Leadership Workbooks
Switch to Holiness Workbook
Unlock Your Full Potential Workbook
Soar to Your Destiny Workbook
12 Power Principles for Kingdom Leaders Workbook

PersonalSanctuary™ GoodTinybooks™
Victory – 30 days of Meditation
Fruitful – 30 Days of Meditation
Success – 30 Days of Affirmations
Influence – 30 days of Affirmations

www.ingramcontent.com/pod-product-compliance
Lightning Source LLC
Chambersburg PA
CBHW051836040426
42447CB00006B/562